# After the Three Moon Era

Gary Fincke

Cover & interior design: Daniel Krawiec

ISBN 978-0-936481-08-1
Library of Congress Control Number: 2015959673

Jacar Press
6617 Deerview Trail
Durham, NC 27712
www.jacarpress.com

# Contents

# Acknowledgements

| | |
|---|---|
| Reports | *Alaska Quarterly Review* |
| After the Three-Moon Era | *The Southern Review* |
| The Difficulties of the Fire Escape | *Prairie Schooner* |
| The Good Silver | *The Gettysburg Review* |
| Watching Californication to See my Daughter's Painting | |
| | *Beloit Poetry Journal* |
| The Geology of Hell | *Chariton Review* |
| At the Angel Museum | *Alaska Quarterly Review* |
| The Conelrad of Apprenhension | *The Laurel Review*★ |
| Ibid | *Southern Review* |
| Weight-Bearing, Balance the Open Stairs | *Silk Road* |
| The Mermaid Cemetery | *Seminary Ridge Review* |
| The Odds | *Serving House Review* |
| The Onset | *Ploughshares* (in part) / |
| | *Cave Wall* |
| Strangers, Falling | *The Gettysburg Review* |
| Tiny Churches | *The Gettysburg Review* |
| Mucklands | *Poets against the War* |
| Loss | *Poetry Northwest* |
| The Inexplicable | *Margie* |
| The Hidden Woman | *River Styx* |
| The Magician's Son | *Associative Press* |
| The Irreplaceable | *Poet Lore* |
| The Scientist in Siberia | *Chariton Review* |
| News | *The Literary Review* |
| The History of Fail-Safe | *Green Mountains Review*★★ |
| The AIDS List | *Poets for Life Anthology* |
| 1965: Charles Manson Tries Out for the Monkees | *North American Review* |
| Basketball at the State Prison | *Smartish Pace* |
| The Illiterate in New Mexico | *Alaska Quarterly Review*★★★ |
| Shooting Eight-Ball in Zhouzhuang | *Mankato Poetry Review* |
| The Peterson Method | *Poem* |
| The Simplification of Cruelty | *Poet Lore* |
| What's Next? | *Valparaiso Poetry Review* |
| Calculations: A Love Poem | *New England Review*★★★★ |

★ In much different form, originally in the chapbook *Handing the Self Back*

★★ Reprinted in *The Best of Green Mountains Review*, 25 Years

★★★ Reprinted on *Poetry Daily*, 2013

★★★★ Reprinted on *Poetry Daily*, 2014

*In memory of my parents*
*and for Derek, Shannon, Aaron, and especially Liz*

# After the Three Moon Era

# THE ODDS

# Reports

On crystal meth, pond snails are better,
tests prove, at remembering pokes
from a sharp stick.  In Afghanistan
some parents use opium to settle
their children.  And there are those who board
each desire as if it were a plane
scheduled for an exotic location;
for instance, the woman on heroin
in a nearby town who, needing
a companion, began to inject
her twelve year-old daughter while the neighbor
bartered more drugs for her preteen body.

A counselor claims the girl, fourteen now,
is healing, observation's evidence
tallied in a fat, confidential file.
Incredible, we say, reading the reports,
thinking the cringing snails must believe
they are subjects of the god of stabs,
that one country's children are at peace.
But yesterday I drove past that mother's house,
slowing to turn and pass a second time,
looking for the terrible accident
of that child.  I might as well have shot
heroin, too, in mime, descending
into a few hours of virtual hell.

And this morning?  A report, with photo,
on the mother's once-striking beauty,
A sidebar on how the daughter, each day,
visits her in prison.  The news that snails
have been turned into tiny batteries
that can be recharged with food and rest.
And furthermore, American children,
studies show, are eating more batteries,
yet nothing makes me learn the how
of these, the when and where, the why.

# The Difficulties of the Fire Escape

That in the beginning they were ladders.
That thousands, once, had balconies made of wood.
That those made of iron would rust to collapse.
That the railings grew hot enough to burn.
That the steep steps were narrow and slick.
That people stored trash on the balconies.
That they crowded them with flowers.
That they led into courtyards without exits.
That they traveled down air shafts that were chimneys.
That they were aesthetically displeasing.
That they lowered property values.
That they reminded tenants of disaster.
That the buildings soared to a thousand steps.
That tenants, now, were terrified of outside descent.
That those skyscrapers filled with sprinklers.
That they were barely flammable.
That such heights were impossible to defend,
And therefore, like gods, they were deemed immortal.

# The Good Silver

The good silver was arranged
In maroon velvet, as soft,
Our mother insisted, as
The inside of a casket.
As if it had a birthday,
The good silver was polished
Once a year, celebrated,
Then replaced, a bequeathed gift
Too valuable to be used.
After its box was opened,
The good silver hummed, some tune
Passed down like the promises
Of Christ. When we handled it,
The good silver burst into
A ballad of burglary,
And we double-locked our doors,
Opened the old histories
Of burials in basements
And gardens, how knives and forks
Were protected from armies.
But when our mother worried
About bills, the good silver
Whimpered its fear of pawnshops.
"Now, now, don't worry," she said,
And closed the good silver's lid.
Just then, our mother, who washed
And ironed our discarded clothes
Before she folded them in
Suitcases we never used,
Walked down the hall to whisper
The shared risks of family,
How even her children might
Unexpectedly suffer.
"Listen," she said, and we did,
My sister and I paying
Attention to the gospel
Of inheritance, standing
In our separate rooms where
Our closets and drawers were filled
With things we would abandon.

# Immunity

*Natural antibiotics are found in all the tissues of the spiny dogfish shark*
— *News item*

The needles that arrive during each dream
Swim in the scrubbed hands of nurses who chant
There now, yes, all right; there now, yes, all right.
Sorcery for the blood, magic for the heart,

These witches' recipes have been prescribed—
Skin of frog, gut of pig, airway of cow—
And here, this morning, the overhead lights
Yellow a monument of water where

Spiny dogfish sharks slide by, natural
Antibiotics in all their tissues.
A school of small children gape and scatter.
I press the glass like a dire infection.

The incurable are foraging through
The animals while all of the places
In ourselves where death begins are humming
The first, faint consonants of genesis.

The long vowels swim up the children's throats,
Held like the routes of medicinal sharks
That turn left, follow two sides of glass, plunge,
Face forward and drive upward to my stare.

# After the Perigree Moon

Even here, in rural Pennsylvania,
a crowd forms near the storage lockers
abandoned by the nameless, dead maybe,
in prison or dementia, missing the rent
for so long nobody sympathizes
when the auction begins, a few dozen bids
thinning the signals until the price stalls
at fifteen hundred dollars, a better gamble
than a few months of lottery tickets.

The moon, last night, was a celebrity, full
and a few miles closer than usual, enough
to bring three neighbors outside near midnight.
One of them suggested *Auld Lang Syne*,
but I was alone with remembering
the approach of planet Melancholia,
how, for one perfect night, it was sized
exactly like the moon, the sky brilliant
with the fascination of malevolence.

A perigree moon, science calls it,
the tides heaving up higher as well.
My neighbors watch televised storage wars,
excited by contents.  Somebody repeats
the story of how eleven hundred dollars
earned a vintage Corvette, and because none
of them has been inside my house, I think
of them bidding when it's foreclosed, what
they'll risk for the things they imagine I keep.

Each spring our village sends trucks to collect
the objects we see as trash—a typewriter,
a VCR, a lawnmower, two grills—
each of those hieroglyphic possessions
spelling what we will not store.  Next week, the moon
waning, a fleet of cars and trucks will invade
our street, the poor permitted to thin our garbage,
value in so many ruined things
that most of the useless vanishes.

# The Primer Route

"Oh look, father," said Jane. "See?"
— *Read with Dick and Jane*

Just after dark, along the Ohio,
We stop for coffee where the attendant
Cannot figure change.  He scatters the coins.
He counts and combines and begins again

While my daughter, the college senior, stares
At cars parking parallel in sequence,
Each driver a skeleton or zombie
Who shouts "Halloween!" and "Death night!" to cheers
From a crowd of short-skirted teenage girls.

Upriver, chemical plants fill a mile
On our left.  We're uneasy with odors
And lights strung holiday-style from building
To building to pipes whose summits are flames.

Above one lamp of pipes, as if we'd passed
Close enough to rub them, a genie seems
So much to form I expect promises,
And the river reverts to darkness, swerves
Right, and we breathe together like divers

Until towers for nuclear power
And chemical, chemical, chemical
Follow each factory logo, the sites
Slung together like the skewed-scale model

For a complex carbohydrate, hundreds
Of molecules bonding into something
Named by prefixes and suffixes and
Numbers to Guiness Book of Records length,
Three thousand, six hundred letters somehow

Necessary as impervious clothes
And self-contained breathing apparatus.
But when she returns to speech, she is Jane
For me, her pleasant father, saying "See"

And "Look," pointing at the primer story
Of those plants as if her mouthing the words
Will connect them to arrangements of ink.
We must be late in the series: Father
Grey at the wheel, Jane in college, polite

Enough to mute her vocabulary
Of effluent and scrubber and filter;
Yet still among them, twenty miles or more,
She murmurs "oh" and "oh," spreading wonder

Down the evening's page like particulate
Matter, as if she trusted the nuance
Of sparse language, its possibilities
Calculated, in small parts per million,
Like the  power of synthetic poisons.

# Calculations: A Love Poem

The billionth digit of Pi is 9,
The last month without a full moon,
February, 1865—
This morning I am making a list
Of the last lines of parables
About the work of numbers, about
Calculations, marking the speed
With which blood travels, as if three feet
Per second were like the blessings
On the late workers in a vineyard
Or a son just home from living with swine.

Someone continues the division
That computes the decimals of Pi—
He is telling a story, numerals
Spilling out toward infinity,
The counting a language, a life
Beyond this one, as difficult
To believe as the number of hours
We've slept together, darkness returning
And vanishing, the moments, nightly,
Between your breaths, the hesitations
In your deep sleep; my own held breath,
Listening, and then, temporarily
Relieved, turning toward the window,
Reciting the autonomic lesson
Of your lungs that swell and shrink
At last, in rhythm, their vital
Capacity, in liters, 3.1.

# The History of Limits

At the doctor's, I choose *Harper's*
instead of *Men's Health, Orion,*
and the Catholic magazine
with the cover art depicting
a haloed, benevolent Christ.
Three pages, I finish, before
a woman announces my name
for a turn with the specialist
and this month's interpretation
of the images of my throat,
his use of "concern," "likelihood"
and "possibility" sending
me to biopsy to define
the adjusted limits of health.

*Once, for the mile run, four minutes,*
*Or otherwise, the heart explodes.*

Last night, from a freeway overpass,
four boys flung rocks until one of them
crushed the face of a teacher riding
to New York.  Curious, they returned,
driving slowly above ambulance
and police. Stupidly, they came back
for a second crawl, earning arrest,
one passenger claiming abstinence
as innocence, the victim measured
critical, myriad of limits.

*Once, for trains, their record speed would*
*Outrun the possibility of breathing.*

Next Friday, the cross-bearers will
re-enact on the April streets
of seven local towns, a crowd
following each of them toward
a temporary Calvary.
The closest martyr, I've been told,
refuses help, hauling his logs
unaided for a measured mile.

*Once, for flight, the speed of sound,*
*Or a man will outfly his voice*
*And strangle on his screams.*

Six hours, now, since a portion
of that teacher's skull was removed
to make room for her swelling brain.
The cross-bearers all wear halos
of thorns, but none of them are nailed.
Leaving the clinic, I return
*Harper's* to its slot. A woman
holds the Catholic magazine.
She does not look up from reading,
even when I pause beside her
to button my woolen jacket,
tempted to tell her that *Harper's*
informed me that German deer still
do not cross the Iron Curtain,
twenty-five years now of the hooved
and vulnerable declaring
their capacity for limits.

*Once, for everything, the speed of light,*
*Or we will disappear into time.*

My father, near ninety, acquired
the querulous voice that speaks through
bolted doors, turning me into
a salesman with a sample case.
After he confessed to sleeping
twelve hours a day, I told him
migratory birds take hundreds
of naps in flight, that some can close
one eye at a time, putting half
of their small brains to sleep, a feat
improbable as Bannister's,
Yeager's, or those future pilots
for whom, Einstein postulated,
time will slow and slow until they
arc back to aged grandchildren
as if they've gained the limitless
advantage of a shaken God.

# Watching *Californication* to See my Daughter's Painting

The painting, my daughter explained,
Is in David Duchovny's bedroom,
Just watch, and when the first nude woman
Rises from the designer sheets,
I follow her body past a wall
Of unfamiliar art.  Somewhere else,
I think, and soon, because he fucks
A succession of women in that bed,
His teenage daughter often nearby,
She, too, sees those women naked,
Entering like a maid, all of them
In that bedroom with my daughter's painting
That doesn't appear in episodes
One or two, David Duchovny
Bedding those women in Los Angeles
Where my daughter lives with her daughters,
Seven and three, who ran naked,
This summer, under the sprinkler
In my central Pennsylvania yard.

I fast-forward through each external shot,
Hurrying toward my daughter's painting
In David Duchovny's bedroom,
The naked woman in episode three
A creative writing student
Like those I teach, nineteen or twenty,
Sliding one step to the side so
I can see the chairs suspended
In the tumultuous blue sky
Of my daughter's rented painting
On either side of that girl's bare shoulders.
She talks and talks until, at last,
She turns into profile, her breast
The focal point of this artless scene,
The painting completely exposed,
Half of the dark chairs silhouetted
By the faint light my daughter allowed
Behind that storm of identical chairs
In David Duchovny's bedroom.

# Weight–Bearing, Balance, the Open Stairs

This week I've read that Methuselina,
The world's oldest ewe, has died in a fall
From a cliff, but fewer American
Children are injuring themselves on stairs.
I'm fifty years, best guess, from becoming
The world's oldest man.  Ten minutes ago
I scaled our three flights to rummage for toys
Before descending as carefully as
A girl in her first formal dress, reaching
My grandchildren who, all day, have scampered
Unscathed on those three brief tests, the youngest,
Four, running up and down like the others.

A local bridge has been condemned and closed,
But yesterday a crowd of neighbors stood
On its surface to enjoy nostalgia,
Their weight estimated at "five small cars."
Our builder, once, the house half done, described
How much stress was being absorbed by beams.
Nearby, a scaffold and winch, a ladder
Someone climbed balancing tools in both hands.

This week, at commencement, a student who
Survived a life-threatening accident
Was wheeled to the temporary platform
Where she heaved herself up, one by one, five
Shuddering stairs, an attendant not quite
Touching her from behind, until a Dean
Skidded a walker to her hands, applause
Following her shuffle to diploma.

Our bones, finally, must carry more than
What's bearable.  We get used to caution,
Yet the frequency of our accidents
Swells like wounds.  More than ever, the number
Of needs for assistance. The sufficient
Are crippled by loneliness. The highest
Of three flights in our house has open stairs.
The youngest grandchild lies on the top step,
Spins, and dangles her thin legs, absorbing
Our terror until she screams and clutches.

# Observing the Future

*Two bottled ghosts, an old man and a young girl, were sold at auction in New Zealand*
— *Harper's*

In the beginning, the bottle winner coddled
     those spirits.
They needed time to adjust to their new home,
     arriving
like the adopted flown from a foreign orphanage
     where fear was
persistent as winter, someone always threatening
     to shatter
those bottles, furious because they refused
     to answer.
The new owner listened for voices. He watched for light
     or even
the faint fog of breath, eager for the temperature
     to plummet
near those bottles. He squinted for small etchings
     to transcribe
as the desires of the dead, the differences age
     and gender
make in the afterlife. At last, impatient,
     he carried
those prizes to his bedroom and lay awake
     in the dark,
pressing the glass to his chest, devoted now
     to dreaming
those bottles uncapped, the incredible brief breath
     of escape
across his face, how that flurry would teach him what
     he'd purchased,
observing the future, tracking the invisible
     to discern
just where the dead disappear to when they are freed.

# The Geology of Hell

She is twirling her hair on one finger,
looking at the floor as if she's spotted
something crawling, as if she is thinking
of allowing it to find her scuffed shoe
and climb, as if she, inanimate, could
never feel six, eight, or a hundred legs.
She is going to scream, I think, right here
inside my office, and I wish the door
wide open as I examine the floor,
finding nothing, and believe, suddenly,
that she is searching for cracks, that she knows,
from online news, that an epidemic
of sinkholes has struck nearby Harrisburg,
a twenty-minute drive, dozens of paved
or landscaped surfaces dropping down like
elevators to forgotten basements.

Listen, I want to tell her, most sinkholes
occur on Thursdays, not Monday mornings.
If you don't believe that, go look it up
and fact-check what geologists have found,
unable to explain it any more
than the geology of hell, but she
is listening for the sound of soil
collapsing outside my open window,
the earth devouring itself, unaware
I am listening, too, for the small faults
groaning  beneath us, her hair still twirling,
the frantic yeast of her hysteria
flaring the one lit lamp into brilliance,
its weather swooning through my torrid nerves.

## At the Angel Museum

Memorials. Stone figures
Disconnected from the names
They've descended to care for.

The wooden.  The gilt cardboard.
The intricate from paper
Shaped for full shelves of wishes.

Just before closing, a bus
Idles in the parking lot,
My wife and I surrounded

By the elderly, many,
I'm sure, younger than we are.
They carry tiny angels

They've created from ribbon
And tissues and directions
Recited by the angel

Who still flutters among them,
Glittery in her gold robe,
Keeping her white wings folded

Like some luminescent moth
At rest, those fragile keepsakes
Taken to Minnesota

Where that bus is housed, even
By the woman who uses
A walker, her pale beauty

Tied to the embroidery
Of her deep-veined wrist.  Eight canes
Rest in an umbrella stand

Just inside the door, and when
I see they're a courtesy,
There is so much imminence,

So close, that the near future
Almost collapses my knees.
And though each  cane has a winged

Woman clinging to its side,
There is such shuffling to where
A pair of haloed women

Hover at the tour bus stairs
That I am shamed by my smile
And flagrantly empty hands.

# The Odds

Sometimes they're determined by the small size
Of the well-protected space at the base
Of the skull where bone ends at the inward
Curve for lessened chance, and yet this student,
A young woman who wrote free-verse poems,
One of which she'd published the week before,
Struck, in falling, that spot so perfectly
Upon the stone edge of a step she died.

For hours, I recreated that tumble.
For longer, I imagined her parents
Who had driven from New Jersey and were
Staying at the president's spacious house,
How their expressions would curse me with guilt.
There was no way to dress for the service
Without concentrating on what horrors
Happen constantly.  My one dark suit seemed
Too light; the pattern in my charcoal tie
Was a sign of indifference and health.

A pastor demanded we call upon
The antidote of hope.  I stood to make
Three minutes of allusions to brilliance,
Unashamed of my brief embellishments.
Her parents, afterwards, spoke haltingly,
Our small conversation complicated
So much by intricacies of absence
That the mother wrapped her arms around me,
The odds of that moment nearly buckling
My knees.  And yes, I steadied my posture
By holding that woman, letting her sob
Into my shoulder, hearing the mourners
Go so silent they could have been straining
To hear which words I breathed into her ear.

# The Conelrad of Apprehension

*In space, scientists say, the Earth's shrieking could be heard*
*— Harper's*

Late in the National Anthem hours,
When channels switched suddenly to snow,
You could stay awake, in 1960,
For the last B-movie of early morning,
And then, before the climax, a final ad
For discount furniture: "Three rooms,
Three ninety-eight" sung by a woman
Who was supposed to be newlywed,
Crooning into her blessed house
From a porch swing as if she'd discovered
The aphrodisiac of contentment.

And next up, Pie Traynor, the white-haired
Hall of Fame third baseman forlornly
Reading his lines beside the boxy way
To heat those marked-down furnished rooms.
"Who can?" a voice intoned from nowhere,
And Pie, from the Hot Corner, answered
"Ameri-can," adding his endorsement
To the history of television ads
Begun by Bulova, 1941, so many,
In twenty years, my mother asked,
"What if they run out of ideas?"
As if counting on them to carry
The lullabies of non-stop programs.

For years now, programming perpetual,
I've flicked through the disconnected
Cable cycle of absence, swearing that
Next would be news of the atomic war.
Time after time I've thought that Conelrad
Was replacing an old comedy
Whose canned laugh track suggested nothing
About the vaporized end of man.
I've followed my fear to a second channel

To make certain that film wasn't the last
Ignorant sit-com in America, somehow
Beaming a lie like three rooms furnished
With tables and chairs anyone would loathe.

Just this morning I've read that the Nautilus
Recalls some useful things for a day, then must
Learn again, discovery returning
Each morning like early television
Or the way we come back to memory
After its threads are worn so smooth it slips
From the hole of usefulness. It's no wonder
The shrieks of the Earth can be heard from space,
Such collective fear slithering from our tongues
As we struggle to recall the language
Of late-night commercials that blink, strobe-like,
In the brain, while we expect our immolation,
Still thinking, during each alarm of snow,
That this is what humility means.

# AFTER THE THREE-MOON ERA

# After the Three-Moon Era

*The dozen fetuses of the sand shark feed on*
*each other until only one is left to be born.*

1

My father sings hymns aloud,
Wakes each morning expecting
To be reborn, telling me three times
As if I'm the genie for death.
He says he hears the brothers
I never had softly talking
In the small bedroom where I slept
While not one of them was born.
They whisper, he says, about the way
He refused them, saying "never"
In the disciplined sign language
Of the rhythm method, keeping
Each of them a jealous spirit.

When he sings "In the Garden,"
I imagine those brothers,
Each day, rising to where my window
Looks out at the rhododendron
Roof-high, the peace of its curtain,
Fragments of light that testify
Like character witnesses
For weather.  They move their mouths
To those hymns that are heavy
With sunrise and resurrection.
Now, in October, the house holds
The early darkness and the dry heat
Of the furnace, and my father
Repeats the chorus, raising his voice
To be heard by those unborn boys
Who wake him each morning like birds.

2

A student tells me she devoured
Her twin in the womb, a doctor
Solving that natural crime
With the spaced clues of ultrasound.

She keeps her shadow twin
Sealed inside a scrapbook
She opens on her birthday,
Leaving the photo face up

In her bedroom.  For when, she says,
Her family sings around her cake.
For when their voices swell
Enough to reach her sister.

3

*Astronomers now believe Earth once had three moons*
        — *Harper's*

Sucked into the sun
or bullied to bits
by the one moon we love,
those other moons vanished
like glittering bracelet charms
sliding off a child's wrist,
the night sky so dim
with places where tapestries
of light might fit, the empty
expanse where those moons
waited to be seen
as beautiful sisters
thrown into the sky
by a jealous god.

4

Once, in Africa, boys ran to their teacher
To tell how their friend had accepted candy
From a stranger's hand and turned into a yam.
"There," they said, "see what's left?" and that teacher
Carried the yam to the police with care.

For thirteen days, nearby, a boy's gone missing,
Turned into nothing but a column of cars
Outside our schools, mothers in silent bunches,
Buses that transport epidemic numbers,
Their red seats emptied by the virus of fear.

Stories are told about boys vanished like time,
Yet returning like swallows.  The police,
In Africa, displayed that yam and people
Flocked to see.  Mothers from nearby villages
Worshipped the hope of metamorphosis,

How their lost children might have been left uneaten
By some candied stranger.  If only they'd been
Transformed into things with voices; if only
They could identify themselves, prove they were
Within some object to be kept and cared for.

5

At his bakery's vacant lot,
my father talks about the missing,
citing Glenn Miller, Judge Crater,
and Amelia Earhart as
we enter the knee-high weeds.
He stands at the memory
of workbench, lays his hands
to the air and carries it
to the bank of ovens.
"Ray Gricar," I say, naming
the disappeared from my town,

his computer in the river,
hard drive removed.
He tells me my mother
is slicing bread, the cash register
behind her, the three of us
working together because
he is icing a wedding cake
just before delivery,
spiraling sweetness so thick
with sugar and lard around
the figures of the bride
and groom, no one should eat it,
trusting me to balance
the three white tiers to the car.

6

Vanishing twins may occur in as many as one of every eight
multifetus pregnancies and may not even be known in most cases.
In one study, only three of twenty-one pairs of twins survived to
term, suggesting intense fetal competition for space and nutrition
In some instances vanishing twins leave no detectable trace at
birth. More than one amniotic sac can be seen in early pregnancy.
A few weeks later only one.

7

Once, my fortune came with a sequence
Of cards. Once, it lay in my palms turned up
To longevity, happiness, travel, love,
Both of the tellers as serious as priests.
Each time I mentioned nothing about how
My daughter had grown into the age
Of ultrasound, one, and then two photos
Of her yet-to-be-born stuck among cards
And snapshots and short lists of things-to-do
On my refrigerator, not telling those seers
My daughter asked not to know their sex,
Her daughters old enough, now, to study
Their early selves like scholars of prebirth.

8

The vanished twin can die from a poorly implanted placenta, a developmental anomaly that causes major organs to fail or to be completely missing, or there may be a chromosome abnormality incompatible with life.

9

My daughter has painted a sky of chairs
That sparkle like redundant constellations.
Her heaven is moonless, the chairs, she says,
Ascending.  The sky bleeds from one side
From the wounds she imagines
On an adjacent panel, one that waits
Nearby, brilliant with light.
Her daughters dream of painting it blue,
A sun shining the chairs invisible.

10

Transformations fill the museum for the missing—
A lunch box, a ribbon, a mitten, one untied shoe.
A boy became a newspaper satchel,
A girl turned into an emptied purse.
We imagine leaves on the tongue,
Mud in the eyes, the sound of weeping
Stifled by blood in the throat.

The morning of the first milk carton child—
Etan Patz, six years old and vanished—
My own three children, ages two to seven,
Ate breakfast as if they were promises
Waiting for a kiss to revive them.

## 11

Simultaneously,
During the three-moon era—
The full moon of joy,
The crescent moon of anticipation,
The half moon of mercy—
Triplets hover
Unseen above
Each late night horizon,

## 12

*Never* arrives with his flashlight,
and you follow to the river
or the woods or the damp basement
of a half-constructed house.
In the morning, you wake
with the coffee maker
set to six a.m., its cough
driving you out of sleep
like a smoke alarm.
Now, when you talk to the air,
somebody is there.
This morning three birds fly
into the living room windows,
one of them dead in the iris,
the other two missing.
A neighbor says it's three flights
of the same bird, but you remember
the music of those thumps,
the variation of size and speed,
and you see the colors
of the missing above the trees,
shades necessary as water;
you stand beneath them, reaching,
your face upturned to spaces
they have left in the sky.

# THE INEXPLICABLE

# Strangers, Falling

*Children universally find clown wall paper*
*frightening and unknowable.*

Each one wears the white face of deletion,
Their baggy suits so uselessly ballooned,
Their enormous shoes spread like helpless sails.
Each evening passes without knowing them,
But some are splayed sideways, skidding across
What seems to be a cloudless wind-swept sky.
Some are seated on nothing, plummeting
From unseen planes.  Or they're twisted, head-first,
Bright smiles lasting to the floor where their legs
Still pedal air, the child, upon waking,
Most frightened by the arms-extended clowns
Who concentrate on improbable flight.

The child asks about sky, where it begins.
At the far edge of everything, he's told,
Where clear weather is always expected.
The clowns, then, must fall from above the sun,
But some mornings he thinks they're carried up
To fall again by an anger of wind
Inside the wall where scratching lives with fright.
When he holds his mouth exactly like theirs
As he stands in his father's floppy shoes,
He feels the floor fall out from under him.
He would disappear if he held that smile;
He would know who they were as he tumbled.

# According to Ibid

According to Ibid, one student wrote,
dutifully acknowledging his frequent,
reliable source whose name suggested
an old, Roman Empire philosopher
so prolific he must have been busy
twenty-four/seven.  Good Lord, this fellow
Ibid must have scratched out a hundred books
by the looks of it, volumes everywhere,
and so varied, what his mother pronounced
a Renaissance man, all those long  hours
in libraries building reputation
until a myriad of pronouncements
could be safely attributed to him.

When he had time, he'd Google Ibid, but
there must be a million hits for someone
he'd cited in English and history,
in sociology and art, Ibid
so wise he fortified every thesis.
What's more, he'd learned that even Ibid had
second thoughts, research rushing over him
like floodwater until he constructed
a safe, new raft of evidence so huge
that whole papers could be a paraphrase
of Ibid, so famous now he was known
by only one name like Bono and Sting,
Madonna and Prince, or any of those
Brazilian soccer players who have been
reverently cited as if their shirts were
emblazoned with the signatures of gods.

# The Mailed Girl

*In 1914, May Pierstorff, four years old, was mailed parcel post*
*for fifty-three cents to save money on her train ticket.*

After I was dressed to ship,
The car clamped jaws around me.
Arranged among the baggage,
I wished I was boxed, shame
Travelling like underwear
And a change of clothes.
Everything inside me was
Neatly packed. In the darkness,
I felt the folds in my heart
Set like wrinkles in laundry
Too long untended.

I learned I could breathe
With nobody in that house,
That fear is a trunk the size
Of a child's closed coffin.
I mastered the art of screaming
To myself.  Parcel post,
I repeated for miles,
Failing to match the rhythm
Of anything I could hear.

When I was hauled from the train,
My lips were so tightly creased
My uncle ran one finger
Over them to feel for stitches.
Two men wrestled that trunk
To the station platform,
The weight of it bringing
Their breath to a boil of grunts.
My aunt murmured her breath
Upon my face to unlock me.
When my uncle carried me
Past that trunk, I could hear
The terrified cry of the mailed.

# Tiny Churches

The claims came on postcards—
World's tiniest church, a photo,
The address above where, in script,
Women wrote "Barely could squeeze in"
Before affixing two-cent stamps,
Sometimes visiting three of them
During one Iowa trip,
Measuring the length and width,
Fitting families in a pair
Of pews, cajoling prayerful
From every face for snapshots.

And yes, I've listened to a guide
Who lived next door to one such church,
Who invited my wife and me
Into her dining room gift shop
To admire small replicas
For a collection she believed
We were forming, my wife patient
Near mugs with chapel decals.

And yes again, we've visited
The best bet for smallest, seating
For two, less than twenty-nine
Square feet platformed in the center
Of an Oneida lake where,
We learned, a minister, bride,
And groom wedged themselves inside
For world-record ceremony
While guests surrounded them
On a small flotilla of boats.

And yes, recently in Yuma,
Where nothing greeted us but
The woman who said, "Too late
For that," the church destroyed
In a storm, her husband announcing
"Microburst" as if he'd been trained

For television weather
On a tiny, closed–circuit station where
Every storm was local, where
Each natural death was news.

"Hardly a drop fell," he said, "just
The terrible wind," the four of us
Standing under a cloudless sky,
The heat set at one hundred twelve,
Dark glasses required. "So rare,"
The husband said, "a burst like that,"
And they walked us into absence
Where we crowded together
At the site of a storm so small
And accurate, we bowed our heads
When they gripped our hands and whispered.

# The Natural History of First Things

*The spacecraft Planck is the coldest known object in space,
including dust and gas*
— *News Item*

About Planck, the space ship, traveling months
On a mission to measure what remains
Of the Big Bang's transformational light.
About that ship, by now, the coldest thing
In space, near absolute zero, its name
Making me look up Planck, the physicist,
His theorem I memorized in high school
The year of my coldest morning, minus
Twenty-two, walking hatless to the bus
In tennis shoes and varsity jacket,
Regretting my terrible vanity.

About relearning Planck's Constant, fumbling
Again with what it signifies about
The causality principle, neither
True nor false, but an act of faith that Planck
Subscribed to.  About that namesake spaceship,
Millions of miles from here, equipped to show
The origin of ourselves, instruments
So perfect they could, from my yard, detect
The heat of a rabbit upon the moon.

About how it's minus two this morning,
Hardly memorable, but cold enough
To open the middle school doors early,
Silencing the chatter of the preteens
Who gather to smoke on a nearby street.
About rabbit tracks in overnight snow
That begin and end at the thick tangle
Of honeysuckle that borders my yard.

About how I imagine the rabbit
On the moon, the probe that could dive bomb it
Like some inter-terrestrial falcon.

About how Planck will detect what remains
Of that original light when only
Temperature existed, tracking theory
To the bright beginning of everything
Displayed as the merciless exhibit—
The Natural History of First Things—
The solid sky plunged into light that lasts,
We're told, forever, so close, now, to God
Or absence, we watch the chilled readouts for
The precise moment of revelation.

# Mucklands

*A local farmer's tractor sank completely under the ground*
*in the area known as the mucklands*
*— News Item*

In May, the morning the President
Is given a tailhook landing,
There are scatterings of flags along
Our drive to the local news, horns that blare
"Mission Accomplished" like a banner.

We park and walk, drawn by the tractor
Said to have sunk beneath a field,
Something impossible as the end
Of war, these things too large to vanish.

The farmer stands among reporters,
Waiting, we think, for rescue's odd proof.
We hear him saying, "Yes, I drove it,"
Answering like the President,
Wearing an outfit that looks so much

Like a rural flight suit, we want
To know how many farmers warned him
Before he entered the drowning field.
"A good place for bones," someone mutters.

We inch closer, testing our weight,
Emitting a chorus of silence
As if limp arms and legs might appear
At the end of the straining cable.

In front of us, the muck turns heaving.
Regret hisses across the surface.
The tractor lifts into light, exhumed,
And somebody guesses its weight
And the circumference of its tires.

On our radio, returning home,
The President preaches, counting on
The short memories of our country.
This afternoon is school, its test
To write an antidote for shame.

# Loss

After his stroke, the wedding singer
Couldn't recognize a song, not one
From those six hundred receptions
Where he'd crooned "Earth Angel" and "Blue Moon"
As often as the address of his house,
What he'd found, once, blindfolded, sensing
The length of three blocks through the drift
Of his Pontiac in neutral,
Turning between two curbs, parking
One foot, four inches, hand-measured,
From his Frank Sinatra mailbox.
He didn't know "Sincerely"
Or "The Way You Look Tonight."
He blinked and wept like the fathers
Of brides, astonished at the end
Of something, failing, even, the test
Of "Happy Birthday" the way
Another set of victims
Loses the use of numbers,
Not knowing what lies between
Three and five or the total
For two plus two, each of them
Puzzled by the plain and simple
Like my mother repeating
"Count your blessings" while she swallowed
Six kinds of medicines, able
To sum the good things, filling
My thirty-six unused high school
Tablets because I'd never written
In them, certain I'd forget nothing
I heard in a thousand lectures,
Since what mattered surely stayed,
All of it said so often
I couldn't lose it if I tried.

# The Inexplicable

*"Childhood apraxia of speech is the inability to turn the mental plan to speak into the necessary physical movements for sound."*

This boy, we're told, spoke for six months, forming
The early sounds for father and mother
And the names of pets before retreating
To silence, hoarding all the common nouns
And verbs, relying upon grunt and gesture
Like the wild boy found in Romania
This week, reunited with his mother
After three years of being raised by dogs.

Not wild at all, this Pennsylvania boy
Who poses with Thumper, his new puppy.
His father cites a magazine that says,
"Oceans have become too noisy for whales,"
Trying to form a cause for locking up
The embellishments and qualifiers,
Stuffing metaphor in some secret room
Behind a crowded bookcase that conceals,
Perhaps, a minuscule spring within one
Of its fifty million words, his parents
Speaking each one, scratching furiously
At the long, unsophisticated code
With the extraordinary coin of hope.

# The Hidden Woman

*Unknown woman found crouched in homeowner's closet*
*— News Item*

I didn't have to invent the woman
Inside my closet, the one and only
Who's earned this headline in the newspaper,
Making my address the most map-quested
By a hundred drivers who have queued like
The awestruck at celebrity viewings,
Thinking *Why was he chosen, why this house*
*So nondescript?* tempted to knock as if
My closet might already be roped off,
The pants and shirts a permanent display
Featuring sleeves that touched her face, the cuffs
That brushed her shoulders like tentative hands.

Listen, because it stores the daily things,
That bedroom closet is always open.
The police?  They'd never touched a woman
Unresponsive beneath a stranger's clothes,
But they made sure she wasn't a neighbor
Or anyone whose car was parked nearby
Like a missionary's, though there, for each
Of those officers to see, was the grass
I'd tracked inside, the tiny tufts of it
In front of that closet door where I'd danced
The brief box step of surprise.  Look, I knew
What they were thinking: Had I encouraged
Her fear by blocking that door?  And what's more,
Would I, after they led her away, dress
In the best of those shirts that fondled her,
Slow with the buttons, my fingers brushing
My stomach and my chest, tucking that cloth
Into pants she breathed upon for hours,
Warming them like a lunatic valet?

# A Citizenry of Birds

*Tarantulas leave behind footprints of silk*
*— Harper's*

My neighbor, shortly after sunrise,
Says he loves to hear English
In the morning from his backyard birds.

They're citizens, he tells me, born here,
So many generations
With us, their accents have disappeared.

His mouth flexes.  The pink horizon
Has nearly vanished. We are
Surrounded by the bright eggs of May.

My nod, meant to be neutral, narrows
The distance to empathy.
Only our lawns show the paths of shoes.

Suddenly, along our street, houses
Are raising flags, becoming
The embassies of allied countries.

When a siren opens full-throated
On the nearby county road,
I try to translate its accident.

Squalled from his architecture of leaves,
Vowels seem a needle's cry
Seeking a sample of suspect blood.

Some of the letters cannot be sung;
His lawn displays the sparkling,
Bent admission to his blue-rimmed door.

46

# The Mermaid Cemetery

Someone tends these graves.  Someone carries kelp
And seaweed to vases brimmed with water
We test with fingertips, learning the salt.

So damp, the pages of the brochure curl,
Its history smeared across photographs
Of the dead who are buried beneath us.

And yes, we find ourselves fools for longing,
Following the mulch trail among headstones
Shaped like fish, becoming witnesses who

Wish ourselves mourners, willing to accept
A measure of loss in order to be
Transformed, bodies returning to water,

Scales swallowing our skin until we fuse
Into the elusive beauty of myth,
Light and land abandoned to those in love

With the possibilities for language,
So scattered below the surface, we would
Be impossible enough for worship.

# The Magician's Son

*If a living being breathes ether, the body becomes as light as a balloon.*
*— Robert-Houdin, magician*

In the first, fascinating years
Of anesthesia, inflated
By medicine's sudden magic,
I returned again and again
To the near-death of ether.
My father taught me to dress
Properly to float, and the truth
Was the buoyancy smell always
Spread from behind the curtain
Rather than the bottle passed
Empty beneath my nose.
My father said the audience
Was suspended, too, between wonder
And disgust, all those fathers
Considering the limits
Of sacrifice, relieved each time
I awoke from my buoyancy,
Blinking as he dropped me back
Into the familiar world.
I stood and walked stiffly
In the suit he'd constructed
For trickery, looking, I knew,
To be so lamed by gas
That fathers, from their seats,
Imagined putting their sons
At such risk, miracles who could
Suddenly die. Always, there was
A collective holding of breath,
Fear wafting over all of them.
Though it might kill him, what father
Doesn't want his son to fly?
Look, after the ether era,
He never again showed such care

And tenderness.  Height became
Ordinary without the framework
For flying.  My upstairs window
Was a mouth through which I thrust
My head.  And yes, I loved looking
Straight down, leaning at the waist.
The trembling.  The anticipation
Of screaming.  My body balanced
By the assurance of an odor.

# The Scientist in Siberia

*Il'yaIvanov worked for years to create an ape-human hybrid*
*— Elephants on Acid and Other Bizarre Experiments*

Like a husband longing for a son after years
Of trying, I followed my chimpanzees closely
For a change in grooming patterns, posture, habits
Of eating. But after nothing took, when those chimps
Stayed barren, what else could I do but advertise
For young women to carry a hybrid to term?

Look, isn't the impossible what we long for?
For them, I drew a dozen dreams of their children,
And when I walked those women to the just-cleaned cage
To start that first blind date, I evaluated
Their expressions for a sign that science, at last,
Could trump the squeamish reluctance of our species.

Always, jailed in Siberia, I imagine
That birth, waiting to see what emerged in order
To name the stranger I'd carry to christening,
Godfather now, standing for that first-of-a-kind.

If only that child could have been taken to term
One of the women who answered my ad become
The mother of a fresh, fantastic race, her name
Throughout the early chapters of New Genesis.

And if that mother was despondent, the father
Returned to the life of somebody who expects
To be cared for? Nothing's unusual in that.
I believed in creation, unlike the father
Gibbering nearby, as if already upset
By the forgery for which he had no language.

# Closets

This morning, waking at four-fifteen, the night light ominously flickering, I see my shoes, six pair, lined up in the closet as if I've died, my suits ready to be bagged for charity. The street sweeper's approach seems so much an army invading I part the drapes an inch to look. One desperate car slides by, running the stop sign like a practicing suicide.

The cleaning woman's vacuum tracks still follow the other side of the bed, ending at the closet where the soul impersonator lies way back behind the robe not worn in thirty years, beside the varsity sweater boxed fifty years in the place that's never cleaned, waiting to be discovered by the next owner the way I discovered some mushroomed darkness under the refrigerator in my first furnished apartment, its fine hair like worthless legs, something to brush into a dust pan, looking away as I dropped it down the drain and ran hot water as if scalding would erase the chance of it crawling back into my future.

In my boyhood bedroom there was a cardboard battlefield where soldiers were slotted for firefights, standing, kneeling, and prone, all of them with weapons raised and aimed at caricatures of Nazis. Some nights, blood wouldn't stop shouting over the sound of firing. Some nights the rain muddied that field, a flood of wounds washing toward where I lay listening to the future that retreated, each morning, into the closet where my cousin's clothes waited for me to grow into them.

By the time light repairs the wound from which sadness seeps, this is merely waking, hearing the first birds who call from the windowsills and gutters because yesterday the backyard birch, the tallest tree on the street, was taken down and mulched. A golf tournament, live, is on television. The players wear coats; I am naked in the heat.

I am afraid that terrorism is passé. I am afraid the war is boring. I am afraid to be in love with the lascivious beauty, heartlessness.

# News

After her daughter disappears.
After the police.  After the priest.
After an hour-long session with the one
Professional counselor in the town,
She calculates the rapist odds,
The lottery of stranglers, follows
The likely chance of sex and drugs.
She chooses items from the drawers
In her daughter's room, imagines
How each would look with blood—stockings
And sweaters, panties, slips—each thing
So suddenly heavy her arms
Begin to quiver from their weight.

A neighbor tells her he walks, each evening,
To the same spot along the river,
Watching the sky from the brush-choked bank
Because a throat through time empties
Into the water, because whoever
Has escaped from a distant horror
Is hurtling toward a darkness splash.
She watches him climb his steel ladder
To his leaf-clogged gutters.  She follows
The tight tumble of rain-soaked leaves
And steps inside to inspect the news,
Staring at the crime and accident crowds
From Harrisburg and Philadelphia.

Once, while a mayor made promises
From where a Korean shop had burned,
Her daughter was nearly there.  Once,
She was almost at the curb when
A comic, holiday balloon passed by.
She keeps dental records in a folder.
They're filed with photographs that
Account for three different styles of hair.
Her neighbor has shown her photographs
Of the river's magical location.
In each of them an upstream bridge
Is so close to salvation she stares.

# THE ONSET

# The Onset

*Bitten*

The first moment screams crippled.
Hurt ovals its small, cramped mouth.

Previous health vanishes,
An unleashed dog, the owner

With his sack of cheap candy
A silhouette at a Halloween door.

Winter's end is a season of shots.
Memory yammers while

I shuffle to the elevator
That rises to where syringes grow

Like the green onions my father
Salted like hard-boiled eggs.

March withers until its shadow goes out.
Each night the grins of animals enter

My room like memorized prayers.
They rhyme their breath with mine, reciting.


*At Midnight, on my Birthday*

My mother, dead at my age, unclasps
Her beaded purse as if entering
My house requires a ticket.

For twenty-four years, she says,
She's carried the proper ID
For pain, waiting to hand it over.

She's dreamed my body
Crippled in yesterday's underwear,
My breath caught in phlegm's thick web.

In a doubled brown paper sack,
She's brought twelve pounds of pennies
Gathered from sidewalks and carpets.

She asks me to arrange them in rolls
For the teller she knows by name,
The woman who lost her husband

At Normandy.  She shakes my clipped hair
And nails from her purse, spelling my name
With her finger in the thick dust of me.

Only after she knows the exact sum
Of her savings does she allow me
To moan my symptoms.  Lie down, she says,

So I can love you.  In two places,
She ties her green gown behind me.
There, she says, now finish undressing.

And yes, she examines me,
Saying, "Relax now, close your eyes.
This is where the past ends."


*Nerve Damage:*

One kind of damage can generate an array of symptoms—
sensitivity, pain, tingling, burning, numbness.  Another kind
produces weakness, muscle atrophy, twitching, paralysis.  There
are causes from probable to unlikely: trauma, compression, poor
nutrition, lupus, MS, diabetes, cancer, ALS, Guillane-Barre
Syndrome.  Treatments vary.  So do results.  There is the chance
of spontaneous recovery.  In one of three cases, the cause of nerve
damage will remain unknown.

*The Onset*

The near future has flushed
His mood levelers.  He knows
I've double-locked my doors.
At eleven o'clock, with news,
He speed-dials my number
For the sex of spoken threats.

Tomorrow, he says.  Imagine.
The following day, much worse.
The bodies of dead friends shuffle
Through the evening solitaire,
The clot of the next hour forming
In the deep veins of my leg.

Caution blinks on, a timed light
In the living room of early-to-bed,
The near future so close by now
He can overhear my breath
As he steals to the window where
The drapes leave a space for an eye.

Of course he loves me lying down,
But when I begin to stand, he adores
The softened chest of hesitation,
The flaccid penis of the small,
Unsteady steps.  So excited
By the stooped beauty of decline,

His eye pressed against the glass
Like a decal of desire, he finds
Himself with his hand, my shuffle
So slow he has time to climax
As I limp brilliantly from one
Night light to the next, exotic.

*Appointment*

In the waiting room, three sets of crutches,
A wheelchair, and some awful barrow that
Holds a man with no legs and a language
Exclusively of vowels he uses
On the tropical fish in the corner tank.
I try to be afraid for all of them.
When I stand, unaided, I am envied.
When I take tentative steps, jealousy
Wheezes behind me.  I walk through a door
Before I stoop and gasp.  I press both hands
Against the wall until ache's discomfort
Replaces the electricity of pain.
Now it is my story again, the one
With a whimper.  Through that wall my fingers
Can almost hear a bellow of vowels
That restart my fiery legs, the ones
That fight the shared posture of deletion.


*Vicodin*

Vicodin may be habit forming.  It may tempt others, so keep it
secure.  Tell your doctor if you drink more than three alcoholic
beverages per day.  Vicodin may impair your thinking and
reactions. Side effects are fainting, confusion, fear, seizures, unusual
thoughts.  An overdose will harm your liver. The first signs of
overdose are nausea, sweating, confusion, weakness.  Later there
is stomach pain, dark urine, yellowing of the skin.  Take Vicodin
exactly as prescribed.  An overdose can be fatal.


*Incubus*

What wakens me is dust bursting
From my back like an incubus.

I am afraid to reach behind me.
The darkness licks its fur, grooming.

Outside, one house is bright so early
It must be lit by carelessness.

The bedroom is a clock.  The phone
Displays a predator's heartless eye.

My mother is not walking off her pain,
An etching in the guest room.

My father is not collapsing
To a gurney.  And I am not

Tumbling down the stairs, so careful
With descent that I can repeat

One set of pains for weeks before
Something worse replaces it.

My father reminds me to walk
Backwards down the stairs, to live alone

So no one knows.  His knees whisper
Until he smothers them with his hands.


*Therapy*

Every movement is a child's, knees near the chest, six variations of
stretching to the jazz of optimism, each riff so simple it terrifies.
Now the octave is pitched high enough to shatter.  In the next
room, a woman moans while waiting.  Weeks from now paces by
the display of canes.  Months from now sleeps sitting in a chair.
Years from now, in stays and corset, swoons into the spine.  When
the legs flutter like insect wings, the room thrums.  Distance is
inches. Self-pity's caught breath nearly shrieks.

*What to Expect*

Standing builds a clot of pain
Behind the eyes where
What to expect gobbles memory,
Unbuttoning its loose shirt
Until its belly unfolds like
Swollen dough, its sex so secret
I have to kneel to know it.

In the neighborhood abandoned
By desire, prescriptions are
Recycled like bottles and cans.
A chorus of "As Needed"
Is sung by a boys' choir
In alto and soprano.

My mouth dries from the darkness.
During the night I wake though
The dead never promise
I can touch their wounds.
Now I am the neighbor watched
From windows, the name for whom
I've become chosen from the list
Of uncomfortable words.

In the stooped world each thing
Has a shadow, the exact
Addresses of childhood as haunted
As prayers for meals and bedtime,
The verses for sickness and sin
Whispered into folded hands.

*Epidural*

An iodine wash. A bee sting. Some pressure followed by a wash
of warmth through the legs receding into relief, it's hoped. Side
effects? Not many and so remote. The worst headache of your
life, not life threatening. Sudden dizziness and weakness, a worse
alarm. A number to call for further instructions. Now it's twenty-
four to forty-eight hours, on average. Up to a week for some. If
you are unchanged, there's surgery, the last resort of the knife.

*Shrinking*

The morning when my bare feet, numb
Through sole and heel, cannot recall
The small wounds of the wooden floor.

The house expands to hold
The unanswered riddles
Of rubbish— receipts rubber-banded
In boxes, stacks of them, year by year.

The yard's roots are aroused
By neglect.  Supported
By a cartel of weeds.
Disintegration barks, a stray
Marking its territory.
At its top, the weeping birch
Dies off into a wispy promise.

Strangers begin to ask
Each other, "Who goes home here?"
When ants cover a plate
Of sweet crumbs, their joy
Ripples like the silent
Marriage of wind and sand.

If a man fears walking,
He hears a match struck
Outside his locked door.
If he leans heavily
On the kitchen counter
He sees the prowler
Near the garage.
If he pours water into a glass
Watching over the lip
As he swallows, he knows
The stranger is deciding
How much he is worth.

*Surgery*

The back muscles, because they run vertically at the incision, can be moved instead of cut. After access is gained, the nerve root is gently moved, disc material removed. Though the success rate is more than 90%, some patients have a recurrence of pain. As for any surgery, there are risks and complications: a dural tear, bleeding, infection, incontinence, nerve root damage. The last two are quite serious, but they remain rare.

*Step Down*

My mother, unaided, walks to the bed
Where, an hour later, she will die.
My father falls from his wheelchair,
Both behind doors, in the dark,
Choosing privacy over rescue.
And now, during one more episode
Of secrecy, I mow my lawn shirtless,
Testing how long routine can last.

Once, a man coaxed me down
From a roof, his breath on the back
Of my neck. "Step down," he said,
And refused to touch me. Step down,
As if faith could be taught, the muscles
Believing in the future.
More than a few minutes
It took to let go, only his breath
Keeping me buoyant.
Without one more word between us
But the shameful need to descend.
The grace of motion refuses to die.
The muscles are louder than the soul.

# REENACMENTS

# What Keeps Us

Before the Civil War, before
The proliferation of bodies
And great distances to ship them,
Embalming was rare, love and grief
Tending the dead's descent into earth,
The bodies keeping their stilled blood.

Antietam, Gettysburg, Bull Run—
Now it wasn't weather's fortune
That extended preservation,
But arsenic, cheap and common
And capable of poisoning
Those who learn history from earth.

Whiskey, likewise, sustained the dead,
Their bodies drunk for decency,
And last night, among the yearbook
Photo display of "classmates passed,"
I found Janet Price, decades dead,
I knew, from love of alcohol.

I settled for remembering
Her small spectaculars of touch.
I ordered mixed drinks, embalming
Myself against anxiety
And fear, and later, bowed my head
Throughout the silence the living
Agreed upon, preserving her
And the rest with recollection.

Next door, a class years younger danced
Under swirls of color that blinked
In sync with the pulse of disco.
A gate-crasher from their future,
I loitered in the doorway while
Two women squinted at my name
To make out which one of the boys
They'd loved had prematurely aged.

Nothing, it turns out, will keep us,
Not even triple-sealed, rust-proofed,
Bronze bunkers guaranteed to rise
And float through catastrophic floods,
Surviving a million years, found,
At last, like alien fossils,
The excavated mysteries
Of permanence pondered by those
Who are left to imagine us.

# Boys' Choir

Always, before we sang,
Miss Quigley gathered us,
saying after the Bomb,
after the fire next time
or barring that, after
heart attack, cancer, stroke,
all of us would be free
of our bodies, the vague,
invisible feather
within us reforming
as our ideal selves who
would sing in harmony.

In the next life, she said,
you will become voices,
all of you a boys' choir.
In the next life, listen,
you will be eight years-old
for a thousand years, nine
for a thousand more, ten
forever, beautiful,
smooth, eternally sweet
altos and sopranos
in paradise.
                And then,
after we filed on stage,
after we were arranged
in quiet, measured rows,
after the stage was lit,
and our surplices glowed,
Miss Quigley beamed and raised
her gloved hands to begin
our preview of heaven,
shrill, young, and shimmering,
so gorgeous as we sang
our enchanted sermons,
oracles for promise.

# Acquiescence

It's been a quarter century since
My story about Ken Blankenship
Stuffing bananas in the mailbox
For our black postman was rejected
By an editor who specified
He couldn't publish an "acquiescence
To racism," my narrator, meaning me,
"Doing nothing but sleepwalking through
Twenty pages of proximate slurs."

And it's been half a century since
I listened to my uncles, who fought
The Nazis, tell my father he would
Regret Negroes in our neighborhood,
Warning him to be watchful each time
Nearby houses were for sale, switching
From "coons" to "coloreds" when they saw me
Eavesdropping through the half-closed door.

That editor who scolded was right
About the autobiography
Behind that early story. I lived,
In 1968, with seven
Other students, and when Blankenship,
Outraged because his girl friend's letter
Was late, jammed the mailbox, I did nothing
Except, a week later, steal his cube steak
From the refrigerator, pleased
To swallow that heavily salted meat.
Though even then I couldn't claim eating
That cheap steak a formal protest, not
Half-drunk past midnight, not running
Scalding water over the greasy plate
And stacking it where all of us kept
Our carelessly cleaned dishes, concealing
A crime so small it was barely shameful,
So easily admitted that I might
As well have confessed, even though any

Of the other six could have stolen
That gristly meat, or like I had done,
Cleaned up the mess those bananas made
After the mailman squashed them beneath
His shoes, scrubbing with my back to the street
So I could imagine I was being
Re-evaluated by a stranger.

It's become a long time since the last
Of those three uncles died, still adamant
About race. "Otherwise," my father said
After each death, "good men," expecting me
To acquiesce to that excuse for them
And for himself. Look, I agreed each time,
Despite that editor's caution, and I refused
To change one word of that story, smug
When some other editor praised
How it used the Martin Luther King
Assassination to expose even
The narrator when the mailman stood
Shouting among the crowd of black faces
Outside the house we rented, flinging
Three bags of burning trash our way before
They retreated from the frantic threat
Of our landlord's brandished shotgun.

For all of the time since then, nobody
Has threatened my house with race or arson,
Giving the grace of re-examination,
Time to evaluate the ease of theft
And avoiding argument, the number
Of pardons I've betrayed, remembering
The expletives and cheap certainties,
The explosive consonants of curses
And slurs I might as well have spewed myself,
Excusing the ignorance of family
Out of what I called love or acquiescing,
Perhaps, to a terrible absence of love.

# The History of Fail-Safe

So tightly coiled, the new way to say "point of no return" became a spring.

We repeated the word with reverence.
We knew what cursing this God could bring us.

Its Bible backed into our lives, tail lights blinking,
then darkening, its make and model mystery.

Hymns were written, all of them prayers that no one sang,
afraid they would lead our fear into temptation.

Our locks were the kind with extended bolts.
Inside our shelters, we slid the short chains
into the slots that sighed reassurance.

Somebody whispered, "Mutual assured destruction."
"What?" we asked. "What?" But the phrase lay dormant in our blood
with the necessary poisons we breathed and swallowed.

We studied Latin's declensions, the inflected
endings for case.  In May, we wore togas to class.
The Romans had worshipped gods dressed like us.  To learn
Russian would have shown the world we were terrified.

When the Conelrad scream spilled from our speakers,
we counted to twenty, anticipating
*This is not a test.*  "Now," our teacher told us,
"everybody knows what it's like to be old."

The old yearbooks were nostalgic with mustard gas
and artillery; they joked about hand-to-hand.
The seniors, for homecoming, carried stones and clubs.
The juniors slung bows and arrows across their backs;
the youngest students armed in another building.

In the stadium, in the fourth quarter,
all the coaches listened to the chugging
of the two-word cheer. The line of scrimmage
dug a trench into the turf. Strategy
was born through the C-section of evening.

While we celebrated in the gymnasium,
apprehension crawled underground in Nevada.
After it disappeared, everyone could still see
its fat ass squirm, indelible as the landscape.

Stand-off was playing on the radio again,
an oldie already, as dated as doo-wop.
We pointed at the sky like toddlers, our fingers
forming the weapons with which we conquered playgrounds.

Fail-Safe turned so red, it glowed like a sore.
Fail-Safe sat in bars until closing time.
Fail-Safe grew fat, breathed heavy on the stairs.

One morning we felt dizzy and our speech began
to fail. When we sat down, starting over, we lost
our legs to the polio of uncertainty.

Every pilot tested the scarred-white wrists of the future. Their
instruments explained precisely where they were, about to say "When."

When the insects emerged, when there were
no shoes and beaks in their baffling skies,

they chittered and squealed among themselves
as if alarm had left their language

since science had briefly entered them.

# Three Stories

*Five*

The cookie in my granddaughter's
Self-illustrated book has long hair
Cut into bangs so much like hers
I say, "The gingerbread man is a girl,"
But she explains he's wearing a wig.
Her cookie escapes the kitchen
To run and play, but on the last page,
That gingerbread man is trapped
Inside the three-dimensional,
Pop-up mouth of a scarlet fox,
The wig gone in the final picture,
Lost, perhaps, in the struggle,
And when I ask why he's smiling
As he's being swallowed, she says,
"Because he only has one face."

*Eight*

Her older sister has drawn twelve pages
About a princess who needs to be saved.
She's locked in a red-brick tower
For a dozen sunny days, her hair
Tightly curled and long, but nowhere near
What would welcome a prince to climb.
One line per page, this princess sings
An abridged "Over the Rainbow."
Bluebirds dot every clear sky,
Lemon drops sparkle, then fade,
But as she finishes, the prince, arriving
On horseback, applauds and stays
Mounted, the rest of the story,
She whispers, a secret-secret.

*Thirty-Seven*

Their mother, no longer afraid
To agree about how giving birth
Introduces the worst fear we know,
Tells about how, at sixteen, she rode

For weeks in David Dixon's fast,
Expensive car. "He killed the next girl,"
She says, explaining everything,
"And just going to the movies."
She means her daughters, five and eight,
The probabilities they're facing,
But he's dead, too, what she's learned
From trolling the Internet
For his life. In another country,
One where nobody travels,
As if he had been a criminal,
As if he had been disposed

# The AIDS List

At breakfast, the AIDS list,
A magazine cover of faces.
On the front porch, a possum
Half-grown and dead, the cat
Looking from kill to me before
Dodging *The Peoples' Almanac*,
Heavy enough to make me killer,
Drawn to my door by the screams
Of schoolchildren, expecting
Chipmunk, rabbit, mouse, bird—
The slaughter list, something like
The ones on the flapped-open page:
20 Illegitimate Children;
12 People who Disappeared
And Were Never Found, though
Patty Hearst, I know, returned,
And so will the cat with more bodies,
Feathered or furred, gifts from the genes
Like DaVinci, Dumas, Strindberg, Wagner,
Four of the twenty love children,
The cat squalling its list
Of complaints from the shrubbery
As if commemoration was
Enough, as if it was insurance
For what we think we know.

# 1965: Charles Manson Tries Out for the Monkees

Like Stephen Stills.  Like Harry Nillson.
Not making the cut, sent packing.
And those bitter years that followed?
Watching television, there was
Plenty of time to cement a grudge.

We all know where disappointment led—
We're left with Manson's solo album,
The one I lifted from a bin
At Heads Together Record Shop.
And then I put it back, saying *No*

To that sort of collecting despite
The five dollars it only cost.
My son, four years–old, stood beside me,
Willing to listen to anything
I played, even the self–produced.

But even unheard, that album
Repeats itself like the awful plots
Of slasher movies, II, III, and IV,
The ones with the point–of–view shots
Through the killer's eyes, the rest of us

With our backs turned or our eyes closed,
Thinking about the upcoming day,
The hours just ahead when we will be
Meeting our families after work
Or relaxing in our homes with friends.

# Basketball at the State Prison

The felons run a layup drill,
Half of them jamming two-handed
To whistles and cheers.  We're playing
At Western Penitentiary,
Everybody black in the gym
But the guards and us, faculty
From a state university.

Their starting five, a guard tells us,
Averages twenty years to life.
The huge center split a man's skull
With a cue stick; the quick point-guard
Pistol-whipped a priest.  I smile and shrug,
Keep shooting like I'm doing time.

They take it to us, those rapists
And thieves.  Short-timers, we stay clear
Of the paint, never take a charge.
Twelve seconds left, seventeen down,
I launch a high-arc, three-pointer
That settles so clean through the hoop
I hear a ripple of "right-ons."

I nod and hand-check the gunman,
The horn bringing us to handshakes
Before his team disappears to
The brief contact of relatives
And lovers, my team on its way,
Within minutes, to cars, a drive
Across town while the radio's
Weatherman details the snow storm
Through which those other visitors,
An hour from now, will be plowing.

# The Peterson Method

Recently reported, an Alaskan brown bear
Scratching its face with a barnacled rock, the first
In forty years seen using tools, though it's been more
Than that since my father-in-law handed me tools
For Christmas, and still more, unwrapped, for my birthday,
Because, he told me, I could find none in your house.
Back then, it was a Svalbardian polar bear
That clubbed a seal in the head with a block of ice,
Prompting a neighborhood watch for the next bright bear
Who converted a branch into cane or weapon
Or a simple derrick for burrowing insects.
My father-in-law expected me to staple
The daily use of tools to my life, the wrenches
Sized and arranged for tasks I wished away like trolls.
He gave me a drill bit with a handle that spun,
Pointed out which steel applications would prevent
The tumors of my house from metastasizing.
Like handwriting, he said, start simple and stay neat,
Inspecting each room as if it was a letter
To perfect while I carried his wife's soft suitcase
To the spare room where, unused, nothing yet had failed.

My father-in-law, dead twenty years now, is stored
As neatly as his furious, unopened tools.
But once, the first time I plugged in electric shears,
I sliced through the slack extension cord, astonished
At silence and how easily error found me.
There was nothing to do but unplug and carry
That accident to my wife who looped the letters
For replacement across her Sunday shopping list,
And for twelve years now, unobserved, I've taken down
Branches and the incessant invasion of weeds,
The second cord intact, hung in careful ovals
Like the early steps of the Peterson Method,
Employing the perfect practice for maintenance.

# Shooting 8-Ball in Zhouzhuang

On this patched table, the pockets too tight, the games stretch like extra-inning baseball. There's a moment, chalking, when I think the last rack might never end, the slow cut curling left where the floor dips, the bank shot stopping short from a soft spot on the rail.

Without one wall, we're nearly in weather so humid I wipe the house stick across my t-shirt before I nearly miscue, calling up chatter from the Chinese fans, twenty by now, who murmur for every Chinese and American miss or make.

Outside, the tour bus to Shanghai idles, and I run, finally, the last five balls, kissing the eight so sweetly down the rail a sigh flutters around us like the pair of storks stirred our way by tourists who pass in groups along the nearby Grand Canal.

# The Simplification of Cruelty

*In India, for centuries, the Thugs worshipped a goddess*
*of terror by strangling their victims slowly, mangling*
*their corpses, and pouring sugar on their graves.*

The teacher's manual said by rote and by rod and never turn your back.  The principal cited the murder of Etta Barstow, stoned to death by thugs she kept after school one hundred years  before a tenth-grade boy used the rock of his fist on the woman who taught history in the room next door to mine. "You have a baby in there?" he screamed, smacking the pillow of her stomach until her "ohhhh" became an end stop for the short sentence of second chances.

Later, three teachers who double-locked an office testified both doors were open until the police arrived, but right then the hallways seethed with students while I stutter-stepped under an ache of lights and opened another door that belonged to teachers, standing in the sweetened darkness as if I wanted whoever waited there to lift hands to my thin throat because I'd stood guard for the vigilantes, supportive as a teen extra in those movies where one teacher gets assaulted or raped, another quits after a breakdown just before the students start to love their book learning, before they sing and dance a tribute to someone who survives.

Inside, in that dark, I wished more than one baby dead, dropping so early they could be the red frogs of miscarriage.  To put us out of work, I wanted to use the bent coat hanger of rage to scrape clean the coming world, and then, switching on the ceiling lights, I stripped off the coat and tie I'd matched that morning and regretted not laying my fists to that boy's stomach, forcing air from his mouth in a staccato of moans while I recited my burial dream, including salutes by numbered guns to mark the old work of violence, their shots arced like the thrown sugar of thugs.

# The Illiterate in New Mexico

After I failed calculus, my father,
A maintenance man, asked me if I knew
The story of how janitors were hired
In Alamogordo, New Mexico,
Whether the name of that town meant something
Or if I'd stopped thinking altogether
About anything but my present self.
"F," he hurled, "is your failure," and I said,
"The atomic bomb" before he shouted,
"If you couldn't read a word, you were hired,
An illiterate in New Mexico."

We were together in a restaurant.
I was as old, within days, as the bomb
And was supposed to become a doctor,
Not clean up after their accomplishments,
Somebody who'd never know their secrets,
A failure sweeping up in ignorance.
All I'd ever be was a patient; all
I'd be able to do was listen while
The way my life would close was decided,
An illiterate in New Mexico.

The scientists, he said, were creating
The end of the world while those janitors,
Excluded from their secrets, emptied trash.
Lips moving, he calculated a tip
Before sliding three quarters and two dimes
Under his plate, waiting for me to stand,
Leaving my grades open on the table
Because I needed to understand that
Anyone, even a goddamned busboy,
Could recognize I was as helpless as
The illiterate in New Mexico

# Subsidence

It's not the atomic bomb, subsidence.
It's not the end of the world, the shifting
of foundations, the cinderblock cracked
where corners of houses keel over like drunks.

It's not fallout, the despair that covers
homeowners in the helpless housing plan
built over the long-closed, anthracite mines.

It's not a firestorm that ruins these roads,
not a shock-wave that creates refugees.

It's not my father inside the fire hall
huddled with his neighbors.  It's not
his hands that straighten the map
where his modest street shows so large
he believes it's a river.

It's not cancer in every family. It's not
decades of dying, nobody returning,
not ever, not even to the half-life
that they endured, measuring themselves
by mortgages that outlive them.

It's not the apocalypse.  It's not news,
watching while my father walks his hallway,
calculating slope with his body, leaning.

# What's Next?

The last time I visit my father
While he still lives alone, he tells me
His longtime neighbor's son is dead, shot
By a stranger on the back porch
Of the yellow-brick ranch I can see
From the three-paned bedroom window.
"About your age, that boy," he says,
Meaning sixty, his neighbor as near
To ninety as my father, the son
Living at home as if he still walked
To the school bus stop with textbooks.
"They say he shot the other man first,"
My father adds, making mystery,
Saying the survivor was found
In the kitchen by my father's friend
Come home from blood tests meant to adjust
The dosages that extend his heart.
"What's next?" my father says. "What's next?"
The answer, for now, his moving
Next week to a nursing home where
What's next will not be his leaving
The stove on or falling down the stairs
Or forgetting a day's worth of drugs.
In his back yard a storm-felled tree
Sprawls so close to the house the door
Can't be opened. The television
Shows darkness, and my father says,
"You try" as if I might resurrect
The guests he watches until he sleeps.
The weather inside his locked windows
Suggests a ceiling of thunderheads,
But he buttons his sweater, closes
The green drapes like a magician
Ready to remove the felled tree
That stretches the width of his yard,
Telling me his neighbor confronted
The killer in his kitchen, saying,
At last, "Where I've sat a hundred times,"

Beginning to remember the shape
And color of the chairs, how a clock
Is hung above the window that looks
Out on the porch, how, if you lean
Over the sink, you could examine
The length of it for your son after
A bleeding stranger nods that way
As if he's answering the question
That you cannot lift into the light
With your just crippled lips and tongue.

Gary Fincke is the Charles Degenstein Professor of Creative Writing at Susquehanna University. Winner of the 2003 Flannery O'Connor Award for Short Fiction, the 2003 Ohio State University/The Journal Poetry Prize, the 2010 Stephen F. Austin Poetry prize, and the 2015 Elixir Press Fiction Prize for recent collections of stories and poems, he has published thirty books of poetry, short fiction, and nonfiction, most recently *A Room of Rain* (stories, West Virginia, 2015), *Vanishings* (essays, Stephen F. Austin, 2015), *The History of Permanence* (poems, Stephen F. Austin, 2011), a memoir, *The Canals of Mars,* from Michigan State in 2010, *Sorry I Worried You* (stories, Georgia, 2004), and *Amp'd: A Father's Backstage Pass,* a nonfiction account of his son's life as a rock guitarist in the band Breaking Benjamin (Michigan State, 2004). His work has appeared in such periodicals as *Harper's, The Paris Review, The Kenyon Review, The Georgia Review,* and *Ploughshares.* Twice awarded Pushcart Prizes, recognized by *Best American Stories* and the *O. Henry Prize* series, and cited fourteen times in the past seventeen years for a "Notable Essay" in *Best American Essays,* his essay "The Canals of Mars" was reprinted in *The Pushcart Essays,* an anthology of the best nonfiction from the first twenty-five years of the Pushcart Prize volumes.